TAKE UP AND FOLLOW

Investigating the Life of Jesus in Luke

Lifeway Press®
Brentwood, Tennessee

ISBN 978-1-0877-6712-3
Item 005838117
Dewey Decimal Classification Number: 242
Subject Heading: DEVOTIONAL LITERATURE / BIBLE STUDY AND TEACHING / GOD

Printed in the United States of America

Student Ministry Publishing
Lifeway Resources
200 Powell Place, Suite 100
Brentwood, TN, 37027-7707

We believe that the Bible has God for its author; salvation for its end; and truth, without any mixture of error, for its matter and that all Scripture is totally true and trustworthy. To review Lifeway's doctrinal guideline, please visit www.lifeway.com/doctrinalguideline.

PUBLISHING TEAM

Director, Student Ministry
Ben Trueblood

Manager, Student Ministry Publishing
John Paul Basham

Editorial Team Leader
Karen Daniel

Writer
Jay Watson

Content Editor
Kyle Wiltshire

Production Editor
April-Lyn Caouette

Graphic Designer
Shiloh Stufflebeam

TABLE OF CONTENTS

INTRO

The book of Luke is not merely a collection of stories about Jesus and His followers. Luke meant business. He captured names, dates, and places with great detail. He had eyewitnesses that confirmed what actually happened and the way it happened. This isn't a casual book. Luke was specific, detailed, and purposeful in every word he wrote. Luke was an investigator.

It is with this purpose that you should pay attention to what Luke wrote about Jesus, and what Jesus asks His followers to do. Jesus spoke about heaven, hell, repentance, and judgment. Jesus performed miracles and argued with religious leaders, often in the same day. Jesus taught in ways that no one had ever heard before.

But Jesus wasn't doing things just to impress people and draw crowds. Jesus demanded His followers give up everything, just as He would give up everything. He called them to take up their cross and follow Him. Little did they know that Jesus would actually take up a cross Himself.

Jesus called His message "the good news." This good news is that Jesus came to save all the people of the world from their sin, not by right living, but by faith in Him alone. Jesus also calls His followers to go and share this good news to all people in all nations.

Be warned: if you read this devotion and commit to reading the book of Luke, your life could be changed forever. You might be called to give your life to Jesus, take up your cross, and share the good news with those around you. Know this: it would be the best decision you have ever made.

GETTING STARTED

*This devotional contains thirty days of content, broken down into sections. Each day is divided into three elements—**discover, delight,** and **display**—to help you grow in your faith.*

discover

This section helps you examine the passage in light of who God is and determine what it says about your identity in relationship to Him. Included here is the daily Scripture reading and key verses, along with illustrations and commentary to guide you as you learn more about God's Word.

delight

In this section, you'll be challenged by questions and activities that help you see how God is alive and active in every detail of His Word and your life.

display

Here's where you take action. This section calls you to apply what you've learned through each day.

Each day also includes a prayer activity at the conclusion of the devotion.

Throughout the devotional, you'll also find extra items to help you connect with the topic personally, such as Scripture memory verses, additional resources, and interactive articles.

THE BEGINNING

SECTION 1

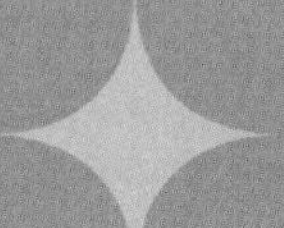

The birth of Jesus, the Messiah, had been promised throughout the Old Testament. For thousands of years, the people of God anticipated the coming of a Savior. The start of Luke gives the deepest exploration into the early life of Jesus that we have. His account reveals truths and helps us know the Savior who God had promised and the people had awaited for generations.

DAY 1

FACTS

discover

READ LUKE 1:1-4.

So it also seemed good to me, since I have carefully investigated everything from the very first, to write to you in an orderly sequence, most honorable Theophilus, so that you may know the certainty of the things about which you have been instructed. — Luke 1:3-4

Sometimes what you find on the internet or on social media can be difficult to trust. You wonder if someone edited the footage or is making things up. It can be hard to know who or what to trust.

Most of the things we know about Luke come from his writing in the book of Acts and a few other places in Paul's letters. We know he was not an apostle with Jesus but became a follower before Paul. He is mentioned in Acts chapters 16, 20, and 27 as well as a few other Scriptures. We also know that he was with Paul until the end, according to 2 Timothy 4:11. Luke was a medical doctor. He was both intelligent and educated, and from the evidence we have, we know details mattered to Luke.

Luke used the words "carefully investigate everything" and "orderly sequence." His Gospel was not an effort to only capture a few cool things Jesus did; Luke was on a mission to tell exactly what Jesus did in the most truthful and factual way he could. He carefully investigated the facts, the dates, the moments things happened, and the names of the people who were there. Luke did this for a specific reason: he believed Jesus Christ to be the Savior of the world. Luke wanted his friend, Theophilus, to be able to trust in the specific details of the life of Jesus. In these few verses, Luke made it clear he wanted his readers to know they could trust this letter to be factual.

delight

How can you be encouraged by the attention to detail that Luke gave to recording the events around the life, ministry, death, and resurrection of Jesus Christ?

How does trusting God's Word challenge you to obey God in your daily life?

Luke was a medical doctor, skilled at paying attention to details. What are some ways God could use your natural giftings for His glory today?

display

Try to remember the earliest significant moment in your life that you can. Maybe it was a birthday party you kind of remember, or maybe a costume someone made you that you loved to wear. Jot down a few details and facts—whatever you can come up with. Then, go ask your parents or a loved one who would have also been involved in this memory for as many details they can remember, and compare their memories with your own.

Now, consider what Luke did and how significant it is for your faith journey today. How has God used the events recorded in Luke to change your life?

Talk with God about the truths you know about Him. Now ask God to remind you of the truths you know you are called to obey. Think about a few things you know about God, and compare them with the things you are called to do. Finally, ask God to show you the ways He could use your talents like He used Luke's talents.

DAY 2

THAT'S DOUBTFUL

discover

READ LUKE 1:5-24,57-80.

"How can I know this?" Zechariah asked the angel. "For I am an old man, and my wife is well along in years."
— Luke 1:18

There are a few instances in the Gospels where angels show up. An angel came to both Mary and Joseph, and despite their fear, they believed and followed the path the angel laid out for them. Today you read a story where someone did not believe. Being a priest, Zechariah was a man known to be very faithful to God. He and his wife, Elizabeth, were both true believers. Regardless, when the angel appeared to Zechariah, he struggled to see beyond what he thought was possible.

Luke 1:9 describes a special moment for Zechariah: he was chosen to be the priest who went into the temple of the Lord. This was a high honor and something that didn't always happen in the lifetime of a priest like Zechariah. Then, after entering this sacred ground, an angel of the Lord appeared to him. These two rare events alone should have shown Zechariah that God had something big in store for him. The angel told Zechariah that he would have a child. Yet, even with all the signs and wonders, it was still too difficult for Zechariah to believe something he never thought would happen. He worshiped the God of the universe, but having a child at his and his wife's age seemed impossible.

This child would be John the Baptist, the voice that would cry out for Israel to "Repent, because the kingdom of heaven has come near" (Matt. 4:17). Zechariah learned that nothing is impossible for God.

delight

Zechariah's words gave away his level of faith in the angel's words. Why do you think this was so difficult for even a righteous man like him to believe?

What are some areas in your life you struggle to trust God with?

display

In the space below, take a pen and draw a straight line. You are going to create a timeline that shows a few things. At the beginning, put down your birth. Next mark a spot where you became a Christian. If you've done so, add a mark where you were baptized. Add some unique moments where you know specifically that God moved in your life. Now, think about a few things that you struggle to trust God with right now. Compare your trust in God with His faithfulness to you. How does God's faithfulness help you to trust Him with the hard stuff too?

It is possible you are working through this book to investigate Jesus for yourself and you've not come to faith in Him yet. If this is the case, create your timeline indicating the important moments that have happened in your life. Look at it deeply. Is it possible God was moving in and through those events in your life to draw you to faith in Jesus?

Make a list about all the great things God has done. Remind yourself of His love, grace, mercy, and forgiveness. Then, ask God to help you today in the areas you don't fully trust Him. Watch your faith grow as you remember God's goodness.

DAY 3

IMPOSSIBLE/POSSIBLE

discover

READ LUKE 1:26-56.

In the sixth month, the angel Gabriel was sent by God to a town in Galilee called Nazareth, to a virgin engaged to a man named Joseph, of the house of David. The virgin's name was Mary. — Luke 1:26-27

Have you ever thought about what it would be like to be in Mary's shoes? She was a teenager who had protected her purity before marriage. Her family had made a commitment to Joseph's family for their marriage and her new life was about to begin. She probably imagined what it would be like to be a wife and mother one day. Everything seemed to be going in the right direction. Then, out of nowhere, an angel appeared!

The angel used some very specific terms that revealed her child would be God's promised Messiah. Mary's question was probably something anyone in her position would ask: "How can I be a mother when I haven't done the thing that could make me a mom?" The angel's answer pointed back to Zechariah and Elizabeth. God had done something amazing by allowing Elizabeth to get pregnant as an old woman, even though she hadn't been able to before. But with Mary, God literally did the impossible.

Mary's response to all of this is truly remarkable. Days before, she may have been daydreaming about what life would be like. Now, all of her dreams would have to change. She chose to trust God with her future, even though it was the most impossible thing she could imagine—God would save the world through her child, the Messiah.

delight

Find two or three specific things the angel said about what Jesus would be like.

Verses 46-55 are often called "Mary's Song." What does this passage teach you about God? What does it teach you about Mary?

How does Mary's faith encourage you today?

display

Think about Zechariah (who we read about on Day 2) and Mary. These were both people of great faith. God used each of them, and they were blessed through His assignment. Did you notice the difference between Mary's singing and Zechariah's silence? Is it possible that sometimes your lack of trust in God keeps you silent? Write down a few ways you can be more like Mary that will help your faith sing!

Small steps of faith can produce great results. The angel told Mary about Elizabeth, so Mary's next choice was to go and see Elizabeth. What step is God calling you to do today?

Mary's song was filled with Scripture. Use your favorite Bible verses as you pray. Let them guide your heart as you celebrate what God has done in your life. Ask Him to reveal how He is calling you to be His servant. Take time and listen before you move on. How are you called to be God's servant?

DAY 4

WHY SHEPHERDS?

discover

READ LUKE 2:1-20.

**Suddenly there was a multitude of the heavenly host with the angel, praising God and saying: Glory to God in the highest heaven, and peace on earth to people he favors!
— Luke 2:13-14**

Have you ever wondered why the angels of heaven were told to sing to shepherds? Why God would choose shepherds to be the first to announce Jesus's birth to the world? It seems a little odd, doesn't it? After all, the job of a shepherd wasn't exactly respected. Their job was to watch animals, keep them alive, and make sure they were fed.

But don't forget, the Bible has many passages about sheep and shepherds. Psalm 23 even describes God as a shepherd. In the time of Moses, God had set up an agreement with the Hebrew people: to atone for (make up for) their sins, they would sprinkle the blood of a valuable and spotless lamb on an altar as a sacrifice. Jesus, the ultimate sacrifice, would be known as the Lamb of God.

Shepherds, sheep, and sacrifices all connect to paint a picture of salvation. Jesus came to earth and did not sin. He was spotless. He came to earth to give up His life for sinners, the lowest of the low. When God revealed Himself to shepherds, it was a way to let the world know that Jesus is for everybody.

The angels declared good news of great joy that God had kept His promise in sending a Savior. Those shepherds took steps of faith all the way to the manger, where they found a baby, just as the angels had promised.

delight

At the back of most Bibles is something called a concordance. Using a concordance or the search feature on a Bible app, find some passages about sheep and shepherds. What do you notice about these passages?

How was Jesus like a sacrificial lamb? How are we like the shepherds on the night of His birth?

If someone were to ask you what "good news" meant, what would you say to them?

display

What might be a modern-day equivalent to a shepherd be in your world (that is, a kind of person who tends to be seen as a lowly outcast)? Would a person in the role you thought of be allowed to enter your church on a Sunday morning? Spend some time thinking about why people are so uncomfortable with others that don't fit the mold. How can you be more like Jesus in this way?

"Repentance" is turning away from sin and back to God. Search your heart to see if there might have been times when you judged others improperly. Think about people in your life you may have been harsh to in some way. Be reminded that your sin has made you just as lowly, yet He offers forgiveness to you anyway. Ask God to make your heart more like His.

MEMORY VERSE

Suddenly there was
a multitude of the
heavenly host with
the angel, praising
God and saying:
Glory to God in the
highest heaven, and
peace on earth to
people he favors!

— Luke 2:13-14

DAY 5

MATURITY

discover

READ LUKE 2:21-52.

And Jesus increased in wisdom and stature, and in favor with God and with people.
— Luke 2:52

Do you remember what it was like to realize you were growing up? Perhaps there was some moment where your toys were less interesting than they used to be; your friends, school, or even the future were things that you found more appealing. Or maybe it was the first time you started to worry about whether you should maybe do something different with your hair. Whatever the moment was for you, we all have a moment where we realize we're not little kids anymore.

There were many moments when Mary and Joseph experienced confirmation that the angels were right: their Son was the Messiah. At the same time, Jesus was just a boy. He grew up like everyone else did. But somewhere around the age of 12, the realization of the fullness of who He was and what He was meant to do were crystallizing in His heart and mind. We don't know for sure, but it's possible this moment was the first time He spoke to Mary about "His Father" in heaven. Jesus was growing up.

Jesus realized His calling and began looking to the future, but His parents weren't quite ready for this moment. They were confused and asked Him to return home. Jesus obeyed His parents, even though they might have not understood what was happening. That chat with Jesus showed both growth and maturity. Sometimes honoring your parents is one of the higher signs of maturity in your spiritual journey.

delight

In a way, Jesus's maturity showed Him standing on his own in a place of worship. How does your personal faith show up at your church? Is your faith your own, or have you simply adopted the faith of your parents?

Think of a few ways you have grown up recently. How have you seen your faith life develop? What are some things you can do to mature in this area?

display

In the space below, make a short list. At the top of the list, write "Growth." Then start numbering the ways you have grown spiritually since you were a child. Now add the ways you are currently growing. Finally, add some things that you believe would help you mature in your faith.

Letting the Holy Spirit guide your imagination, compare your growing up with Jesus's. Think about ways that He might have grown in wisdom, favor, and stature with both God and humans. Ask God to help you to not only grow up physically, but spiritually. Ask God to give you a heart for trusting Him heart, mind, and body.

DAY 6

WILD BOLDNESS

discover

READ LUKE 3:1-20.

He went into all the vicinity of the Jordan, proclaiming a baptism of repentance for the forgiveness of sins, as it is written in the book of the words of the prophet Isaiah: A voice of one crying out in the wilderness: Prepare the way for the Lord; make his paths straight!
— Luke 3:3-4

God never wastes a word in Scripture. When He spoke through His prophets, we find it fulfilled throughout His Word. There are times you might read something and think, "Why?" For instance, why did the angel tell Mary about her cousin Elizabeth being pregnant? Elizabeth's pregnancy was amazing, but why did the angel tell Mary? Because God made a promise that a prophet would arrive who would announce the coming of the Messiah. That prophet was John the Baptist, promised by Isaiah 700 years earlier.

John's message and method was meant to awaken the Hebrew people. They hadn't heard God's voice in 400 years, and now someone was calling them to repent and turn to God. It probably wasn't much of a surprise to John that others wondered if he himself was the Messiah. But John knew his message and calling. He called people to repentance. Jesus would call them to faith and salvation.

John the Baptist was so committed to let the world know, he wasn't afraid to face difficulty from the leaders of the time. John trusted that God had sent Jesus to save the world.

delight

What specifically was John's message to the Hebrew people? Try writing it down in as few words as possible.

How would that message help prepare the people for the coming of Jesus?

How does John's life and teaching encourage you to live for Jesus today?

display

John knew that if he continued to preach about the Messiah and confront the sin of others, he would be punished for it. Take a moment and consider some of the ways you get nervous about actively living out your faith in Christ today. Living for Jesus means rejecting the ways of this world. While no one is asking you to live out in the wilderness and eat locusts, you are certainly called to boldly proclaim Christ to others. What fears are keeping you from being bold today? Write down below a few of those things that make you a little nervous to speak up about Jesus.

Pull out your trash can. Take a slip of paper and write down some fears keeping you from being bold. After you write each one down, crumple it up into a ball and hold it in your hand. Pray to God about that fear. When you are done, toss that fear in the trash. Repeat the process until you've cast all your fears away. Pray for God to give you boldness like John the Baptist.

DAY 7

CONFIRMATION

discover

READ LUKE 3:21-38.

When all the people were baptized, Jesus also was baptized. As he was praying, heaven opened, and the Holy Spirit descended on him in a physical appearance like a dove. And a voice came from heaven: "You are my beloved Son; with you I am well-pleased." — Luke 3:21-22

Lists can be boring and ancient names difficult to pronounce, so we often skip over long lists of difficult names when we read the Bible. Yet, here in chapter 3, Luke spent several verses writing the names of men who had long since died. Why is this here?

In the time of Jesus, there were many people who weren't so sure who this man named Jesus was. So when Luke wrote his Gospel to teach about Jesus, he wrote with precision and clarity. He placed two things next to each other that at first glance don't make a lot of sense: a description Jesus's baptism with the Holy Spirit descending upon Him, and a list of family members.

Both of these details are confirmation of who Jesus is. He was the descendant of Abraham and David, through whose lineage God had promised to bless the world. The list of names helps factually place Jesus in line with these families. In addition, although many people were baptized by John, it was only when Jesus was baptized that the skies opened and a voice from heaven spoke. No different from Mary and Elizabeth, the beginning of Jesus's ministry was confirmed by the Holy Spirit showing up and God declaring from above who Jesus was. Both earthly and heavenly, Jesus was confirmed to be the Son of God.

delight

Quickly read through the list of names in Luke 3. How many names do you recognize? How do these people align with the promises that God made for a Messiah?

How does this confirmation of Jesus's lineage help you to trust God more with His promises for your life?

display

Draw a tree on a piece of paper. It can be as detailed or as simple as you'd like. Write your name on the trunk of the tree, then begin to write names of the people who have spiritually impacted you on the branches and leaves. Finally, underneath the tree, write down the name of the person(s) who led you to become a follower of Jesus. Around each name write a few words that are significant to that person's faith journey. Take a moment to look at your completed tree and see how God has been faithful all around your "tree of faith." This is confirmation in your life that not only is God real, but He keeps His promises.

There are times when every believer in Christ has doubts. One of the key weapons to battle doubt are the times in the past when God confirmed His presence and faithfulness in your life. Ask God to remind you of some of these times. Are there moments you can look back on and see exactly what God has done in your life? Thank God for those instances and ask for help to take steps of obedience and faith from those confirmation moments.

DAY 8

DEPENDENCE

discover

READ LUKE 4:1-13.

Then Jesus left the Jordan, full of the Holy Spirit, and was led by the Spirit in the wilderness for forty days to be tempted by the devil. He ate nothing during those days, and when they were over, he was hungry.
— Luke 4:1-2

Before Jesus's earthly ministry officially began, God led Him into the wilderness for forty days. During that time, Jesus would not eat. His only dependence was on God. The forty days is meant to remind us of the forty years that Israel spent in the wilderness because of disobeying God. Jesus's forty days would look very different. Every temptation Jesus faced dealt with His obedience and submission to God.

Satan tempted Jesus three times: to create food for Himself, to fast-forward His kingdom without having to suffer, and to reveal His power before God called Him to do so. These were all ways Jesus could show that He didn't need to depend on God the Father. "You can make food out of stones." "You can show the world Your power right now." "You can save Yourself." All statements of self-sufficiency.

But every step along the way, Jesus remained faithful. He combated temptation with words from the Old Testament. Satan had a temptation; Jesus had Scripture. He spoke the words of God to help Him stand up under temptation. Hebrews 2:18 reminds us that Jesus was tempted just like we are. His example is one we can follow, one verse at a time.

delight

As you read Luke 4, what are some ways you see Jesus display His dependence on God?

How many Scriptures have you memorized? Write down as many as you know below.

display

Take a moment and consider a few temptations you have faced recently. Can you think of some Scripture that would help you know how to stand up under that temptation? Try to find a few Bible verses for each temptation you face. Now, create a list either on your phone or in the front or back of your Bible that you can access quickly when you find yourself struggling to stay faithful. Don't be shy about this. Print off Scripture and slip it under your phone case. Put it on the dash of your car. Tape verses on the inside of your locker. Jesus proved to us that Scripture can help fight temptation. Think about the best way for you to do this today.

Think about how you want to pray with God today for help, and then do your best to use only Scripture to pray with Him. Use the Bible in all the parts of your prayer if you can. If you can't yet, that's okay; do the best you can. Take the Scripture you read today and pray about some of Jesus's quotes from the Old Testament, still trying your best to use Scripture in every sentence.

THE MINISTRY

SECTION 2

The birth and resurrection of Jesus are two moments celebrated every year by people all over the world. In between those two important events, we discover how Jesus wants us to respond to His life, ministry, teachings, and example. In this phase of His life, Jesus called disciples, taught, did miracles, and revealed the heart of God for people.

DAY 9

BELIEVING THEN SEEING

discover

READ LUKE 4:14-44.

"The Spirit of the Lord is on me, because he has anointed me to preach good news to the poor. He has sent me to proclaim release to the captives and recovery of sight to the blind, to set free the oppressed, to proclaim the year of the Lord's favor." — Luke 4:18-19

When Jesus read the scrolls from Isaiah, He was reading a famous passage about the coming of Messiah. But there's one part that He left off the end of His reading, a part about God's judgment. Why? The reason was that He said what He read had been fulfilled before them. The judgment, however, is something that will come at the end of time.

We don't read much about how the crowd responded, but Jesus knew their hearts. He compared them to two different moments in the Old Testament. The first had to do with Elijah telling a poor woman that her needs would be met in a miraculous way during a famine. This woman believed him; her faith happened before she saw the miracle. The second moment was an example where a man's pride and foolishness wouldn't allow him to immediately see how God had provided. Jesus essentially called out the people for being unspiritual and unwise.

Jesus spoke truth from Scripture, and then He spoke truth to a crowd who couldn't see past their own pride and personal perspective. They had watched Jesus grow up. How could He possibly be the Messiah? He knew that no matter what He did, they would be skeptical.

delight

If Jesus performed a miracle right in front of you, would you believe that it had happened? Why?

How does God's Word help you to combat doubt and cynicism?

How does Jesus's defense of Himself using Scripture help you to know how to defend yourself when people try to tear down your faith in God?

display

Think about someone in your life who is older than you and who you know to be a strong follower of Jesus. When you are able, send them a text or call them and ask about a time when they might have struggled with doubt. Find out how they trusted God's Word when sometimes it didn't feel like they had seen a miracle from God.

Take notes on what they say, and then from their answers, see if you can find two or three things that you can use to help your trust in God and His Word grow.

Take a few moments and write down specific promises you believe God makes in Scripture. Talk to God about His promises for believers in Christ. Ask God to help you to trust what He says in Scripture to be true for your life today. Pray that God will help your faith to grow!

DAY 10

MASTER OF TRUTH & FISH

discover

READ LUKE 5.

When Simon Peter saw this, he fell at Jesus's knees and said, "Go away from me, because I'm a sinful man, Lord!" For he and all those with him were amazed at the catch of fish they had taken, and so were James and John, Zebedee's sons, who were Simon's partners. "Don't be afraid," Jesus told Simon."From now on you will be catching people."
— Luke 5:8-10

One day, Jesus walked up with a crowd following Him. He taught with so much authority that Simon Peter called Him "Master." After hearing about Jesus from his brother and the people around town, and now having heard him teach, Simon Peter was aware that Jesus was different from everyone else.

Peter had spent his life catching fish, so he knew much more than the average person did about fishing. He knew the boat, the equipment, and the weather. So when Jesus told Simon Peter to cast his net out again, he didn't do it because he thought Jesus knew more about fishing than him; he listened to Jesus because he had heard things he couldn't explain.

After Peter caught all those fish—more than any normal man could catch on his own—he realized Jesus wasn't just a master of teaching. Jesus was directly connected to the God who created everything—including fish. Peter's response lets us know he felt undeserving to be around someone as holy as Jesus. Simon Peter had heard about Jesus, listened to His teachings, and finally experienced a miracle himself. This left Simon Peter a changed man.

delight

Go back and re-read Luke 3 and 4. What are a few things Peter would have heard about Jesus?

How do you relate to Peter's response to Jesus? In what ways do you feel undeserving of God's love? How has Jesus helped you to not be afraid about this, like Peter?

display

At the core of Peter was something he had done his whole life: he fished. The job was relentless: You wake up every day and you fish. Sometimes you don't catch anything at all. You still get up and go fishing every day. When Jesus called Peter, He took Peter's special qualities and redeemed them for His purposes.

Take some time and write down some unique qualities that God has given you. How are you specially made to be used for God's glory? God loves you, and if you have given your life to Him, you've been saved. He has redeemed everything about you, including your gifts. How can you use who you are for God's glory?

Use what happened to Peter as an example. Talk with God about the ways you feel undeserving. Ask forgiveness for what you need to, and remind yourself of the ways you have been forgiven. Finally, talk with God about your giftings and how you can be used to "fish for people," just like Peter.

DAY 11

WELL BUILT OR WEAKLY BUILT?

discover

READ LUKE 6.

"He is like a man building a house, who dug deep and laid the foundation on the rock. When the flood came, the river crashed against that house and couldn't shake it, because it was well built." — Luke 6:48

It's one thing to say something is true, but do your actions match your words? Jesus started this famous teaching by asking a question: "Why do you call me 'Lord, Lord' and do not do what I tell you?" (Luke 6:46). He was pointing out a truth that is undeniable: we often say one thing and do something totally different.

There are many people on earth who would claim to be Christians, but deep down, their beliefs end up being far from anything remotely Christ-like. The foundation to a healthy Christian life is submitting to Jesus and doing what He tells you to do. It's not building a house on rocks, but building your house on *the* Rock.

Jesus made the image of a cornerstone—the stone that's foundational to the whole building—practical and personal. If you build your life on the Rock who is Jesus Christ, you will make it through whatever storms come your way.

The end of this parable is brutal. A weak foundation destroys a house, which represents a life. When you build your life on anything other than Christ, the results are devastating.

delight

Why is it difficult to build your life on the foundation of Christ? What things distract you from living this way?

Write down the many benefits that come from building on Christ's foundation. Specifically put on paper some things you have experienced that encourage you to do this.

display

Go to your closet or drawers and grab a bunch of t-shirts. Put the t-shirts on your bed and fold them like you normally would. Then begin stacking the t-shirts, one on top of the other. Count how many it takes for the pile to topple over. Pull a few t-shirts away and start stacking again. Once you feel like you have a nice sturdy pile, take one step back and hop on your bed. What do the t-shirts do? How would this have been different if you'd done the same thing on the floor? Do you see how important a good foundation is?

Ask God to help you to be a person whose words and deeds match. Ask Him to help you know what He is calling you to do and give you the strength to do it each day. Finally, ask God to help you to be obedient to His will.

DAY 12

FAILING TO FORGIVEN

discover

READ LUKE 7.

"Therefore I tell you, her many sins have been forgiven; that's why she loved much. But the one who is forgiven little, loves little."
— Luke 7:47

Imagine one day your teacher calls you in for a special meeting, just you and the worst student in the class. Currently, you have a B- and the other student is failing miserably. The teacher looks at you both and says, "Today I have decided that both of you will get a B+ in this class for the semester." Which student do you think would be happier about this?

It almost doesn't seem fair, does it? One person was failing and now has a terrific grade they didn't deserve. Yet for you, going from a simple minus to a plus changes very little. In a way, that is what Jesus saw before Him. A woman who was "known" for her sin by many people was overwhelmed that Jesus would even speak to her. She wept. She poured expensive perfume on His feet. She wouldn't stop showering Jesus with praise and affection. She was known for her sin, but her faith in Jesus brought her forgiveness. The love she had in her heart for Jesus was overflowing into her life.

The reality is, our sin has earned us all failing grades. We can't do anything to earn the forgiveness Jesus offers through faith. Yet God offers this grace to us anyway. Because of Jesus, we go from failure to forgiven.

delight

In God's eyes, which person had a greater need for forgiveness from Jesus, the woman or the Pharisee? Why?

In what ways have you responded to God's love and forgiveness for your sin? Does your love reflect Christ's love for you?

display

Think about how you could show God's love to someone this week as a response to what Jesus has done for you. Maybe you could give an unexpected gift. Or maybe you could do a job for someone that they weren't looking forward to doing themselves, something simple like cleaning up your bathroom so your parents don't have to, or taking out the trash before anyone asks you to do it. Maybe you could show extra grace to someone at school who you know is having a tough time. Whatever the case, attempt to practice what the woman did for Jesus. Show God's love to someone else out of God's love for you.

Take this prayer time and reflect on the ways Jesus has forgiven you specifically. Get detailed in your heart and mind, and reflect on the ways Jesus has shown you that you are forgiven. In the space above, write down ways that you are thankful for God's forgiveness.

DAY 13

SIGNS AND WONDERS

discover

READ LUKE 8.

The man from whom the demons had departed begged him earnestly to be with him. But he sent him away and said, "Go back to your home, and tell all that God has done for you." And off he went, proclaiming throughout the town how much Jesus had done for him.
— Luke 8:38-39

Jesus healed people of sicknesses and evil spirits. He walked on water in front of witnesses. At one point, He encountered a man possessed by so many demons that the demons called themselves "Legion," and even these demons recognized who Jesus was and the power He held.

In the midst of these miracles, Jesus told a parable and explained it to the crowd. There would be people who would hear Jesus's teachings and see miracles with their own eyes, but would not believe that Jesus was the Messiah. That is a difficult reality to comprehend when your life has been changed by Jesus.

We don't know much about the man who had been possessed. It could have been years since he had been possessed. Yet, we read about him sitting next to Jesus, fully cleaned up and in his right mind. All he wanted to do was be next to Jesus. It makes sense—Jesus had saved him from a life of being a slave to others. Jesus had set him free. However, Jesus knew that there would be no better person to share the good news then someone like this man who was lost and now found.

delight

What natural pattern do you notice in chapter 8 with the people who Jesus saved or healed?

Do you remember your first response after Jesus saved you? What was it like?

How have you gone and told others how Jesus has changed you?

display

You may have more in common with the man once possessed than you think. Write down your story of what your life was like before coming to faith in Christ. Talk about the things that enslaved you. Finally spend some time writing down exactly what you would say to someone about your coming to faith in Christ and how your life is now different.

Thank God for saving you and for the healing of your heart, mind, and soul that comes through faith in Jesus Christ. Ask God to show you opportunities to share your story of good news with others around you. Finally, pray for the people whom God places on your heart. Pray that you will be aware of the moments when you can talk about Jesus with them.

DAY 14

KILLING SELFISHNESS

discover

READ LUKE 9.

Then he said to them all, "If anyone wants to follow after me, let him deny himself, take up his cross daily, and follow me." — Luke 9:23

What does it mean to be a Christian? If you were to ask that question to a few different people, you would probably get some very different answers. Some people think that if you are good and follow God's laws, then you are a Christian and will be saved. What Jesus says in Luke 9 proves that to be untrue. It is faith alone in Jesus Christ that saves—but what does that really mean?

Having faith alone in Christ means that you fully submit to Him in every way. Sadly, we can often be interested in building our own kingdom rather than God's kingdom. Our hearts and minds are led by our selfish desires, rather than by God.

Every day and every moment when you wake up and say, "God, whatever you want me to do, I will do," that is you deciding to let the Spirit kill off selfish thoughts and motivations and allowing Him to change your heart to focus on what God wants for your life. That is what full submission to Jesus looks like.

delight

Jesus asked the disciples who they thought He was. Who do you think Jesus is in your life?

What does taking up your cross daily look like for you today?

display

In past devotions, we've talked about ways God can use your gifts for His glory. We even asked you to write down some of those special talents God has given you. Today, think about some ways your selfish nature might use some of those giftings for selfish purposes. After you've spent time thinking about it, come up with a plan to help you daily take up your cross. Maybe you've already begun by doing a daily devotional, but write down some other specific steps you can take to follow Jesus intentionally and daily.

As you are talking to God today, ask Him to show you some moments when you have made things about you. Ask Him to forgive you and help you to make things right with people you may have harmed. Finally, ask God to give you strength and courage to put away selfish thoughts and turn your mind and actions to living for Him every day in every way.

MEMORY
VERSE

"So I say to you, ask, and
it will be given to you.
Seek, and you will find.
Knock, and the door
will be opened to you.
For everyone who asks
receives, and the one
who seeks finds, and to
the one who knocks, the
door will be opened."

— Luke 11:9-10

DAY 15

HAVE MERCY

discover

READ LUKE 10.

"Which of these three do you think proved to be a neighbor to the man who fell into the hands of the robbers?" "The one who showed mercy to him," he said. Then Jesus told him, "Go and do the same." — Luke 10:36-37

When the teachers of Jesus's time spoke, they often used examples in groups of three. So, when Jesus taught the parable of the good Samaritan, the crowd expected to hear about a priest, then a Levite, and finally a normal citizen of Israel who would be the hero and help the man. The priests and Levites were often despised for the way they not only worked with the foreign government that was ruling over Israel, but also how they often were seen as acting better than everyone else. The crowd wanted Jesus to tell a story of the common Israelite man saving the day. But Jesus did something shocking and chose to make the hero of the story a Samaritan.

The Samaritan people were once Israelites, but they had intermarried with other nations and accepted other religions. They were not only disliked but hated by Jews and those who considered themselves to be true Hebrew people. They saw them as people who rejected God and His law. When Jesus made the Samaritan the hero of the parable, it was shocking to hear.

A person of Israel was in need and a Samaritan chose to show mercy and help. Most certainly at that time, anyone hearing Jesus tell this story would not have expected the conclusion. What this means of us is that our neighbor is any person—including an enemy—who needs mercy.

What does it mean to show mercy to another person?

How have you been shown mercy from others in the past?

How has God shown you mercy?

display

If we define "mercy" in view of what Jesus did on the cross for our sins, then we know that He paid a great price for something He didn't do. More than likely, you don't have a list of enemies like Samaritans. However, we all know of people in our lives who are facing difficult situations and are in need of mercy. Think about actual examples of how you show mercy to others. It could be emotional, an act of service, or even financial. What are some ways you can show unexpected and undeserved mercy to someone today?

Read Romans 12:1-2 and then pray based on those Bible verses and what you learned in today's devotion. Ask God to remind you of all the mercies He has shown you. Spend time in prayer, praising God and allowing Him to renew your mind. Finally, ask God to reveal to you moments where you can show mercy to others.

DAY 16

ASK. SEEK. KNOCK?

discover

READ LUKE 11.

**"So I say to you, ask, and it will be given to you. Seek, and you will find. Knock, and the door will be opened to you. For everyone who asks receives, and the one who seeks finds, and to the one who knocks, the door will be opened."
— Luke 11:9-10**

Have you ever wondered what it would be like to be one of the disciples who followed Jesus in person? They saw everything. In your reading today, the disciples watched Jesus pray. He talked to His Father right in front of them. They had all prayed to God before, but the way Jesus prayed must have been different from anything they had seen before. They wanted to pray like Jesus prayed, so they asked Jesus to teach them.

Jesus taught them the Lord's Prayer, and then He explained to them the attitude they should have while praying. God has proven His faithfulness throughout the history of the Hebrew people. The promised Messiah was standing right before them in Jesus. Because of this, Jesus told His disciples to continually ask for God's guidance and goodness in their lives. If they would keep asking, keep searching, and keep knocking, the door would be opened.

God is good, and He wants us to know and understand Him. Therefore, we have to do just like Jesus instructed. We have to keep on asking, keep on seeking, and keep on knocking.

delight

The Lord's Prayer includes many elements, such as praise, confession, and petition (asking for things). Try breaking Jesus's prayer into parts and identifying the different elements that it includes.

How can you use the Lord's Prayer as a model for praying such that you are continually searching and seeking? How can it be a regular part of your prayer life?

display

In the space provided below, write down a few ways you or your faith community have continually prayed for something and saw God move in faithfulness. You don't have to tell the whole story, just a few parts that you can remember off the top of your head. Think of as many examples as you can. Now, take a picture of this page with your phone and save it. If you don't have a phone, just tear this page out of the devotional (after you do tomorrow's devotion). Use this picture or page as a reminder of God's goodness and faithfulness

Take your time today, and one by one, pray through the separate parts of the Lord's Prayer. To start with, ask God to help you understand the parts of the first line. What does it mean to be both heavenly and Father? Pray to the God of the universe, who wants you to know Him on an intimate level. Pray each part of the Lord's Prayer this way as a continual seeking process for your growth.

DAY 17

TOOLS FOR YOUR SPIRITUAL TOOL BELT

discover

READ LUKE 12.

"But seek his kingdom, and these things will be provided for you. Don't be afraid, little flock, because your Father delights to give you the kingdom."
— Luke 12:31-32

We humans are good at worrying about things we can't control. One of those things we worry about is our height. When you are in middle school, many of the girls are taller than boys and they might wonder, "Am I always going to be taller than these boys?" Boys worry about the opposite. Everyone wonders if they are going to be taller or shorter than their parents, siblings, and friends. The ironic thing is that you can't do one single thing about it.

Jesus said that worrying was a complete waste of time. You can't change your height. How do you think worrying about something is going to make anything better? While we all understand this to be truth, it is much harder to practice this truth in real life. God provides for every molecule of life on this planet. Birds, flowers, and even humanity are blessed and overseen by God's authority.

Specifically, Jesus told His followers to replace worry with seeking first God's kingdom in all parts of life. This means taking your focus off of yourself and your own concerns and turning your focus to God and the things He cares about most. When you do this, you find you not only achieve a feeling of joy for be involved in the Father's kingdom, but you also worry less.

delight

What do you think it means to "seek first the kingdom of God"? What are some things you've learned about God's kingdom from your time reading the book of Luke?

If you seek God's kingdom first, what specific things are you looking for? What is then given to you?

display

Design a treasure map for yourself. Draw a giant "X" to "mark the spot" and underneath it write, "No Worries." Leading to the "X," wind a dotted line all across the page, and along the way leave landmarks, spots where you can write truths from Scripture that might help you not to worry. When you think about something that causes worry in your heart, consult your treasure map to help you seek God's kingdom first!

In your prayers today, reflect on the ways spiritual tools have been "added" to you so that you can fight things such as worry and anxiety. Thank God for the many ways He has provided and equipped you with these things.

DAY 18

TINY FAITH. BIG THINGS.

discover

READ LUKE 13.

He said, therefore, "What is the kingdom of God like, and what can I compare it to? It's like a mustard seed that a man took and sowed in his garden. It grew and became a tree, and the birds of the sky nested in its branches."
— Luke 13:18-19

The first portion of Luke 13 shows Jesus being attacked by religious leaders for healing on a Sabbath day. The Sabbath was a day God created for rest and worship. It was meant to show your trust in God by resting on that day and focusing your heart and mind on God. The religious leaders had turned it into a day when they could watch others and judge them. Jesus labeled them hypocrites—people who say one thing but do another.

While teaching, Jesus saw a woman. No one told Him she had suffered for eighteen years, yet He knew. He also could see her faith. When He healed her, He freed her from a life of suffering. Rather than be amazed by all that Jesus taught and did, the religious leaders tried to attack Him for doing this healing on the Sabbath.

This is a classic example of caring more about rules than faith alone in God. Jesus did not come to condemn the world but to save it. He never sinned, yet He gave up His life for hypocrites and sinners all the same. The religious leaders had great knowledge and little faith. In contrast, we know very little about the woman other than her illness and her faith. Her faith was clearly greater.

delight

How do you think faith can be like a seed that grows into a tree?

How have you seen your faith life exponentially grow?

Would you consider your faith to be a seed, a sapling, or a tree? Why?

display

Let's get creative. Imagine what it must have been like to be the woman in the story from Luke 13. Write down a few lines of what you think her life might have been like. Write about her journey just making it to see Jesus despite her disabilities. Write about what she could have thought or felt when she was healed. Finally, write about what Jesus's story on seeds and yeast would have meant to her.

Pray for God to show you ways you can grow in your faith because of what Christ has done in your life. Pray for clarity and direction so that you can let your faith grow into a strong tree. Ask God to give you strength to stay faithful to Him over any rule-based or legalistic ways of living.

DAY 19

COUNT THE COST

discover

READ LUKE 14.

"Whoever does not bear his own cross and come after me cannot be my disciple." — Luke 14:27

When a person becomes the right age, they get to do something they never could before: they become drivers. It's a lot of fun to think about driving a car, but not the most fun to think about how much driving costs. Insurance, car payments, and the simple fact that you need fuel to make it go means that the cost never stops. To drive, there is a cost.

By this time in Jesus's ministry, He was very well known. Even the king of the region had heard of Him. Many knew about His teachings, miracles, and the crowds following Him. They knew He had fed thousands of people from a few fish and loaves of bread. He was quite popular! It was possible that some people just wanted to be close to Him or hear what He said because it was a cool thing to do. Jesus wasn't having it.

"Give up your family, loved ones, money, stuff, and even reputation if you truly want to follow Me." That's the general understanding of what Jesus meant. He encouraged them to count the cost.

Faith in Christ is not a casual thing. Following Christ means giving Him your heart, soul, and mind forever: that is the cost. The result of doing this is life everlasting, experiencing perfection and freedom from sin with God in heaven. Have you considered the cost of following Jesus?

delight

What are ways that you take up your cross and follow Jesus?

What ways have you seen others talk about Jesus but not really follow through?

There is a cost to following Jesus, but there is also blessing and reward. Write down a few of the benefits to following Christ.

display

Calculate how much it would cost you to purchase a car, pay for registration and insurance, and how much you'd need to spend on gas for two years' time. Write down the total.

Look at that big number and think about what it would cost you to cover those expenses. Now, think about what it would mean to sacrificially give your heart, mind, and soul to Jesus. Write down what that looks like and the things you would have to give up or things you have given up. Compare this to your answer on the previous page about the benefits of following Christ. How does the cost compare to the reward for you?

Pray over the list that you made today for the cost of following Jesus. Pray about what it looks like to be a disciple of Christ. Pray for God to give you wisdom, mercy, and the ability to stay faithful as you walk in His grace. Ask Him to help you clearly see the benefit to following Him.

DAY 20

LOST AND FOUND

discover

READ LUKE 15.

"'But we had to celebrate and rejoice, because this brother of yours was dead and is alive again; he was lost and is found.'"
— Luke 15:32

Israel had been God's chosen people for thousands of years. They knew God promised they would be His people. They acted at many times like the younger son in the story, but they always had the love of the Father. There are times when you have grown up knowing something that becomes less significant as time goes on. For instance, if you have a father who loves you your whole life, when you become an adult, it is something you are used to having. You might take it for granted.

Christians know what they are supposed to do: they are called to share the good news about Jesus with the world. This gospel story lets the world know that faith in Christ saves them from sin and eternal death.

Sadly, with time, we can forget how important this is. We can get more comfortable with simply following rules and only being around people who act like us. Because of this, we don't reach out and share the good news with others as much as we should.

Jesus was calling the Hebrew people to remember what God did for them and what He had promised. The message for Christians today has not changed: God cares about everyone so much that He gave His Son for the sins of the world. That's truly good news.

delight

In the story you read today, how did the forgiveness of the father lead the son to restoration?

How has God's forgiveness changed your life?

What are some ways you can grow in telling others the good news?

display

Write down the basics of your story of coming to Christ. Try to remember dates, places, and conversations that led you to faith in Jesus. If God used a message or sermon to speak to your heart, think about what you heard that convinced you to follow Jesus. Now, set a timer, and try to share your story of how Jesus changed you, including the gospel message, in under five minutes. If you want, record yourself on your phone and watch it back to see how you did. How close did you get to five minutes?

Pray that God would cultivate your heart for the lost who you see every day. Pray that God might use the story you just practiced in some short conversation over the next few days. Pray for God to open doors so you can see someone come to faith in Jesus.

DAY 21

MONEY, MONEY, MONEY

discover

READ LUKE 16.

"No servant can serve two masters, since either he will hate one and love the other, or he will be devoted to one and despise the other. You cannot serve both God and money." — Luke 16:13

Do you worry about money? Maybe you've never really thought about it and its not a big deal. Or maybe it's all you can think about. Either way, money can lead to a great deal of worry. Money is something we think controls our future. If we don't have money, we can't buy a car or a place to stay. To go to college is difficult without money. Money itself isn't evil, but placing your trust in money is a very specific form of idol worship. It is interesting to think that money was worshiped even in Jesus's time.

When Jesus mentioned being a slave to money, it sounds a little odd at first. But the more you think about it, the clearer that becomes. You can spend your whole life working, saving, and storing away money. The reason you do this is because you believe it will keep you safe. Ultimately you spend your entire life putting your faith, trust, and hope in money.

Jesus's message is clear: you can not worship both God and money. Only one of these truly has all power and authority over heaven and earth in the past, present, and future. Only one of these can truly save you.

delight

From your readings, write down a few examples Jesus gave of people who loved money and what it did to them.

What are some ways you can protect yourself from becoming an idol worshiper of money?

display

The Bible talks more about money than just about any other topic. This reality can make us pretty uncomfortable. Take a moment and count up how much money you have. It could be a few bucks or it could be thousands; the amount doesn't really matter. Count it up and then pray for God to show you how to give some of it away. Generosity is one of the few ways we can physically show God we trust Him with our lives.

Spend some time talking with God about whether you trust Him or money more in your daily life. Ask Him to help you to be truthful with Him about this. Ask forgiveness if you need to. Ask God to help you grow in the area of generosity so that you can learn how to trust Him with your future and your finances.

DAY 22

SEVEN?

discover

READ LUKE 17.

"Be on your guard. If your brother sins, rebuke him, and if he repents, forgive him. And if he sins against you seven times in a day, and comes back to you seven times, saying, 'I repent,' you must forgive him."
— Luke 17:3-4

In the Lord's Prayer a few days ago, we learned to pray, "Forgive us our sins, for we ourselves also forgive everyone in debt to us. And do not bring us into temptation" (Luke 11:4). Luke 17 feels like an echo of these previous verses. The idea of forgiveness and temptation being connected makes sense. The idea of forgiving others makes sense as well . . . in theory. To truly forgive someone who has wronged you seems almost impossible at times.

It's not so bad to forgive someone we love and have built trust with over years, but what about someone we don't trust? The Bible makes it clear: forgiveness is for everyone. Check out the parable of the good Samaritan (see Luke 10:30-37). We are called to even forgive our enemies.

Do not forget that you were once an enemy to God. What separated you from God was the sin you committed against Him. As God forgave you—even when you were His enemy (see Rom. 5:10)—you must forgive others.

delight

Why do you think it can be difficult to forgive people who have hurt or wronged you?

How does God's forgiveness of your sin motivate you to offer the same forgiveness to others?

display

It can be difficult to find a way to express forgiveness beyond simply saying the words. Words are powerful, but at the center of today's verses is a number: seven. This passage doesn't mean we should forgive exactly seven times; it's an expression that simply means we are to forgive others as many times as we've been forgiven. While you can say the words of forgiveness, another way you can speak forgiveness in someone's life is to show them that you love them. Think of one person you need to forgive. It might even be someone you have already told "I forgive you." Make a plan: for seven days in a row, find a different way each day to show them in some way that you love them. Think about how this exercise can help you to grow in forgiveness toward this person.

Thank God that He no longer keeps a record of your sin but only looks at what Jesus has done for you. Ask forgiveness for things that have kept you from having a right relationship with Him. As you do this, ask God to remind you of ways you need to forgive others. As you are reminded of God's forgiveness, ask Him to help you to do the same for others.

DAY 23

RICH, YOUNG, & HELPLESS

discover

READ LUKE 18.

When Jesus heard this, he told him, "You still lack one thing: Sell all you have and distribute it to the poor, and you will have treasure in heaven. Then come, follow me." After he heard this, he became extremely sad, because he was very rich.
— Luke 18:22-23

There is a reality we all must face: we are hopeless and helpless without Jesus. When we're children, helplessness is a way of life. We need people to feed us, take care of us, and keep us safe. But as we get older, we learn self-sufficiency. The goal of adulthood is to move out and do our own thing. We can forget that ultimately, we still need God.

Jesus had a conversation with a man who asked a question: "What must I do to inherit eternal life?" Jesus offered an answer that He knew would reveal the man's heart: "You know the commandments." Of course, the man not only knew them but had kept them on his own. From an outside perspective, he had done the right things. Jesus knew what he lacked—he needed to realize he was helpless apart from God.

Jesus knew the man loved money and felt far from helpless. He didn't think he needed forgiveness. The rich young ruler thought he had it figured out but couldn't give up the thing he trusted more than God. He could not practice the faith of a child.

delight

What does it mean to be helpless without Jesus?

What was the sin of the rich young ruler?

How does realizing your helplessness bring you towards a greater faith in Jesus?

display

For this exercise, pick out a pair of regular tennis shoes with laces. Walk over to your bed or chair and sit down with the shoes in front of you on the floor. Place one hand behind your back, and without using it, try to put on those shoes and tie them. How did you feel? Compare this to what your life was like before you asked for forgiveness and chose faith in Jesus. Read Romans 3:23 and 6:23, and think about what these verses mean in regard to helplessness.

Declare your helplessness before God right now. Talk to Him about how much you need Him and how you are thankful for His salvation in your life. Pray for Him to keep you aware and sensitive to the fact that you are helpless without Him.

DAY 24

TRANSFORMED FOREVER

discover

READ LUKE 19.

"Today salvation has come to this house," Jesus told him, "because he too is a son of Abraham. For the Son of Man has come to seek and to save the lost."
— Luke 19:9-10

It is interesting to think that both Matthew (one of Jesus's twelve disciples) and Zacchaeus were tax collectors who lived around the same time and place. It is possible they knew each other. Maybe that's why Zacchaeus had decided he must see this Jesus who had pulled Matthew away from the wealth and comfort of being a tax collector.

Zacchaeus was both rich and hated. Even though he was a Jewish man, he had partnered with Rome to take money from the people of Jerusalem. Because of how he was allowed to collect taxes, there was much room to take as much as he could and cheat anyone he wanted. Yet, there he was in the tree, trying to see Jesus. It was Jesus who called him down from the tree and demanded that they go to his house.

One chapter earlier, we learned of the rich young ruler who couldn't give up everything to follow Jesus. This is precisely what Zacchaeus did. If you do the math on the promises he made to pay people back, it adds up to everything Zacchaeus had. This is a helpless childlike faith that transformed Zacchaeus forever.

delight

Compare the "rich young ruler" from Luke 18 to Zacchaeus. What differences do you see?

What would you do if you were Zacchaeus? How would you make amends with the people around you?

display

Sometimes, much like Zacchaeus, changing your perspective helps you to see things differently. You don't need to climb any trees, but it might be good to put yourself in the shoes of other people. How do you think your parents see you? What about the people at school? Do they know your faith? Now, think about the people you know who are lost. Consider how they might look at you when it comes to both your word and deed. Do they see Jesus in your life? If the answer is yes, then how can you reach out to them like Jesus did with Zacchaeus? If the answer is no, then what changes do you need to make today to make Jesus more evident in your life?

Pray that God would give you the heart to call out to the lost around you like Jesus did with Zacchaeus. Ask Him to help your words and actions match up in a way that honors God and helps others see the beauty in Christian living. Pray for strength and faithfulness to do and say the right things for God's glory.

DAY 25

CORNERSTONE

discover

READ LUKE 20.

But he looked at them and said, "Then what is the meaning of this Scripture: 'The stone that the builders rejected has become the cornerstone'? Everyone who falls on that stone will be broken to pieces, but on whomever it falls, it will shatter him." — Luke 20:17-18

In verse 17, Jesus was quoting Psalm 118:22, which is a prophecy from the Old Testament about the Messiah. Jesus was speaking to religious leaders who were trying to trap Jesus with His own words. Jesus knew their evil intent and made it very clear where His authority was from. Jesus also made very clear the results for anyone who rejects Him.

Jesus's parable about the vineyard owner is disturbing and sad. The owner had done nothing wrong. He had built a wonderful place to work and was not only stolen from, but his own son was murdered though he had done nothing wrong. Do you see the connection between the parable and Jesus?

This is a difficult but true reality. Faith in Christ alone brings life. Rejection of Christ brings death and separation from God. This is why we must build our lives upon the cornerstone that is Jesus Christ. Being broken—brought to a place of understanding our sinfulness—by Jesus means He can forgive and rebuild us again. Without Him, we are broken for eternity.

delight

A cornerstone is the strongest foundational piece of any building. How would you consider Jesus to be your cornerstone?

How can you best explain God's judgment for unbelievers at the end of time? How does this make you feel about sharing the good news with the lost?

display

Take a small break from your devotion and take a walk around the outside of your house. Look at the foundational floor and outside walls. If you are able, peak underneath and look at the support beams that hold the house up. Imagine your house without those things. Now compare your foundational understanding of Jesus in your faith life. How can you build upon Him today?

Spend today's prayer time reflecting on people you know who have not given their lives to Christ and who have maybe even rejected Him. If you believe that nothing is impossible for God, then pray bold prayers on behalf of those who are lost and in need of Jesus. Pray that God will show grace to those in need. Ask God for a miracle in the lives of the hard-hearted.

DAY 26

TRUTH THAT WON'T FADE

discover

READ SCRIPTURE.

"Heaven and earth will pass away, but my words will never pass away." — Luke 21:33

Do you ever get scared reading, watching, or hearing about the news of things happening in this world? Wars, sickness, and natural disasters seem to happen all the time. Remember when you had to wear a mask at school? Perhaps you still do. For a while, you stayed at home and did school online to keep yourself and others safe. Did it feel like the world as you knew it was coming to an end?

In Luke 21, Jesus spoke about wars, nations crumbling, and the hardships of things that would come. This is the hard reality of a fallen world: bad things happen. Jesus taught His disciples how to pray and how unproductive it is to worry. He also taught them many truths about God and what He truly cares about.

In a few different ways, Jesus also taught about not putting our faith in money or religious leaders, or putting our faith in ourselves by trying to keep the law on our own. Repeatedly, Jesus called His followers to give up their lives, take up their crosses, and follow Him. His reason was clear: He came to save the lost. That path of faith came through the life and teachings of Jesus. His Words are perfect, true, and eternal. Unlike kingdoms, rulers, and fortunes on this earth, God's Word will never fade.

delight

In Luke 21, what are a few of the things Jesus foretold would fall on earth?

How have you seen Jesus's teachings and truth be everlasting in your life?

display

Anything that happens in the past is history. Write down some historical moments that have happened since you've been born. Think about major events in the world around you, and then think about things on a more personal level. Write down a few of both in the space below. Now compare the ups and downs of your past with the ups and downs of the world. Add to this the things you have learned about Jesus from this devotional. How have Jesus's eternal teachings helped you make it through your history?

Consider the lessons you've learned on fear, anxiety, and trusting God with your future. Ask God to point you to His eternal truths that give you hope in Him alone forever. Pray for His peace as you take every step of faith into your unknown.

THE FINISH

SECTION 3

Up to now in the writings of Luke, we've experienced the life and ministry of Jesus. Jesus's desire was to bring glory to God through showing us how to pray, live, and trust Him. These last four days tell the story of His final days on earth. What He did changed the world forever.

DAY 27

HARD PRAYERS

discover

READ LUKE 22.

Being in anguish, he prayed more fervently, and his sweat became like drops of blood falling to the ground.
— Luke 22:44

We must never forget that it wasn't easy for Jesus to go to the cross. At the Lord's Supper, Jesus brought forth a cup and told His disciples that His blood would be poured out for them. It was only a short time later that He would find Himself talking to God in prayer, saying, "Father, if you are willing, take this cup away from me—nevertheless, not my will, but yours, be done" (Luke 22:42).

This might be as important of a prayer for us to know as the Lord's Prayer. They are similar in what they say, but here we find Jesus praying out of desperation. Not only this, but He meant the words when He said that He wanted God's will for His life more than His own. Could you pray that prayer? Have you prayed that prayer?

This is a great reminder that Jesus was both fully God and fully human. In His humanity, Jesus understood what it was like to face temptation. "For we do not have a high priest who is unable to sympathize with our weaknesses, but one who has been tempted in every way as we are, yet without sin" (Heb. 4:15). In Jesus's divinity, He could pray "not my will, but yours, be done" without any false motive or deception.

Jesus would suffer and didn't deserve to. He knew what would happen, and He still willingly gave up His life for us. This is the beautiful example of Jesus. We need to pray like Jesus, even when it's hard.

delight

When have you prayed hard prayers to God?

What is the "cup" that Jesus referred to in His prayer? Why was this cup so important?

display

Jesus willingly allowed Himself to suffer for God's will to be done. Recall some times where you were struggling with what God wanted you to do. What were a few moments in your life when you knew God's will was better for you than your own wants? Write a prayer that models Jesus's, asking for God's will to be accomplished more than your own.

Praise God for the faithfulness of His Son. Thank God that His plan of salvation through Jesus has existed since the beginning. Ask God to bring you the type of strength that Jesus had so you can stand up under sin and temptation and actively and daily choose to live for God's will.

DAY 28

A BRUTAL DEATH

discover

READ LUKE 23.

And Jesus called out with a loud voice, "Father, 'into your hands I entrust my spirit.'" Saying this, he breathed his last. — Luke 23:46

It doesn't matter how many times you read it, the story of Jesus's crucifixion and death is brutal. For six hours, He endured agony. His body was blistered from the sun, and all the while He was verbally attacked by the people watching. A crown of thorns, the beatings, and the abuse all took place in front of His mother and loved ones. Jesus died by suffocation from fluid filling His lungs. We know this because when His side was pierced, the fluid that flowed out was not just blood. Yet through it all, Jesus did not sin.

This was the fullness of God's plan. The salvation of the world would come through a sinless man giving up His life for the sins of the world. This one-time act of one man dying for all would satisfy God's justice as the penalty for sin. Faith in Christ brings salvation because God now looks at you and sees what Jesus did.

This was the moment Jesus had tried to explain to His disciples, but they hadn't been able to grasp it. He was the Messiah who would save the world, but salvation was delivered in a way they didn't see coming. Jesus had prayed to the point that drops of blood mixed with His sweat. When He entrusted His spirit into the Father's hands, His agony was over. His disciples didn't understand, but very soon God would do something amazing that no one expected.

Why was it necessary for Jesus to die on the cross?

Jesus's disciples were slow to understand His plan because they had a different expectation of what the Messiah would come and do. When has God's plan differed from your expectation?

display

Read 1 Corinthians 11:23-26. Compare Paul's writings on the Lord's Supper to the actual death of Jesus on the cross. Prayerfully consider what Jesus was trying to tell His disciples that night at the dinner table. In whatever way you are able, practice the Lord's Supper at your home. Physically break bread and think about Jesus's body being broken for you. Take the juice and imagine His blood being poured out. It may seem gross or morbid, but the point is to remind you of the great cost that Jesus paid for your salvation.

Thank God for His plan for salvation that was fulfilled in Jesus. Thank Him for His faithfulness and goodness in keeping His promises. Ask God to remind you of what Jesus has done for you and on your behalf. Pray that you would live your life proclaiming what He has done.

MEMORY VERSE

"He is not here, but he has risen! Remember how he spoke to you when he was still in Galilee, saying, 'It is necessary that the Son of Man be betrayed into the hands of sinful men, be crucified, and rise on the third day'?"

— Luke 24:6-9

DAY 29

AN EMPTY TOMB

discover

READ LUKE 24:1-35.

"He is not here, but he has risen! Remember how he spoke to you when he was still in Galilee, saying, 'It is necessary that the Son of Man be betrayed into the hands of sinful men, be crucified, and rise on the third day'?"
— Luke 24:6-9

Put yourself in the shoes of the followers of Jesus at the time of His death. They had the Messiah for three years, spending every day with Him and eating countless meals with Him. They had heard His teachings and even explanations that not everyone else heard. They had not only seen miracles performed; in the name of Jesus, they had also performed miracles. At that moment in time, Jesus was dead. Can you imagine what that must have felt like for them?

Death, however, is only half the story. Three days passed. The sun rose, just like any other day, and they found themselves heading to the tomb where Jesus's body had been laid. They expected nothing more than to weep even more than they had and to care for His body. What it must have felt like to see an empty tomb and hear the words, "He is not here, but He has risen!"?

Jesus not only paid for the sins of the world, but He defeated both sin and death and made a way for anyone who believes to be saved from sin and death. Through His death and resurrection, we are offered eternal life.

What did Jesus accomplish when He rose from the dead?

How does it make you feel to know that God did exactly what He said He would do by sending a Messiah?

Now that you've read God's plan for salvation in Jesus, how should you respond to God's truth in your life?

display

Even though the disciples had been told what would happen, they were still afraid. What are some things that you are still afraid of? Write out two or three of those things. Now, consider what Jesus has done and how He can bring you comfort today.

Thank God for every part of Jesus's story: His birth, life, teachings, death, and resurrection. Thank Him for what you have learned and how Jesus's life brings you hope. Pray that God would help you with your struggles and fears today. Ask God to help you stand strong because of what Jesus has done for you.

DAY 30

YOUR TURN

discover

READ LUKE 24:36-53.

He also said to them, "This is what is written: The Messiah will suffer and rise from the dead the third day, and repentance for forgiveness of sins will be proclaimed in his name to all the nations, beginning at Jerusalem. You are witnesses of these things. And look, I am sending you what my Father promised. As for you, stay in the city until you are empowered from on high."
— Luke 24:46-49

Jesus repeatedly talked about and shared the good news with everyone He met. He also helped His followers to understand that they were called to tell the world of His gospel. This wasn't something that would only stay in Jerusalem. All the nations were supposed to hear of what God had done in Jesus.

This calling isn't different for us today. Jesus has risen from the dead. He is the picture of God's love for the world, and faith in Christ brings the forgiveness of sins and eternity with God in heaven. Even though thousands of years have passed, the calling to share the good news of Jesus Christ hasn't changed.

Anyone who claims Jesus and takes up their cross to follow Him has been called to proclaim what He has done for us. You are called to live a life that shows people what Christ has done in you. You are called to share with your words and your actions that Jesus has saved you and changed you.

delight

Thinking back through all the devotions, from memory, write out what the good news is.

Have you given your life to Christ? How do your words and actions reveal the truth of your answer?

display

Write down four or five reasons that you are called to share the gospel. Also, write down a few ways you feel more prepared to share the gospel because of your devotional readings in Luke. Finally, make a short list of people you want to talk with about Jesus and what He has done for you.

Thank God for all the many ways He has equipped you and prepared you to share the gospel and be bold for Him. Ask Him for strength and courage to talk about Jesus even when it makes you a little nervous. Ask God to calm your nerves and help you remember how eternally significant every faith conversation is. Ask God to remind you that He is with you, and His Spirit guides, strengthens, and empowers your words for His glory.

GOD CAN USE YOU

Sometimes we think we have to be a career missionary, pastor, or leader of a faith-based organization to tell people about Jesus and really make a difference. Luke shows us this isn't true.

By trade, Luke was a doctor. He wasn't a pastor, though he did travel with Paul. He also wrote two books in the New Testament: the book of Luke, which detailed Jesus's life and ministry, and the book of Acts, which chronicled the growth of the early church as well as Paul's missionary journeys. We still benefit from Luke's work today.

What would it be like to leave a two-thousand-plus year legacy of faith? To know God can use us anywhere, in any program of study or career path?

Legacy is just a big word for the kind of story we leave behind about who we were. A legacy isn't built all at once, but in little moments and decisions over time. Use the following acronym to help you make decisions that leave a legacy of faith, like Luke, of living for God wherever He places you.

L — How can God use me to show ***love*** to the people around me right now?

E — How can I live my life with ***eternity*** in mind?

G — Who around me needs to hear the ***gospel***? How can I share it with them?

A — What ***actions*** can I take to serve those who don't know Jesus?

C — What can I do to build up others in my faith ***community***?

Y — What is God inviting me to do, and what would it look like to say "***yes***"?

Now, using this acronym and the questions next to each letter (p. 108), write out where you are on your legacy journey right now. Then spend some time in prayer, asking God to show you how He can use you to influence others for Him for years to come.

L —

E —

G —

A —

C —

Y —

THE GOSPEL IS FOR EVERYONE

In theory, we know that the gospel—the message of who Jesus is and what He has done for us—is for everyone. However, when it comes to who we actually tell about Jesus . . . maybe we're a little more selective. Maybe we're more comfortable talking to strangers about our faith. Maybe we're most confident about sharing our faith with family. Or maybe we're most excited about sharing the gospel with people we find attractive or want to date.

Using the circles surrounding the main bubble in the bubble map below, write a quick description of the people Jesus ministered to who stood out to you most.

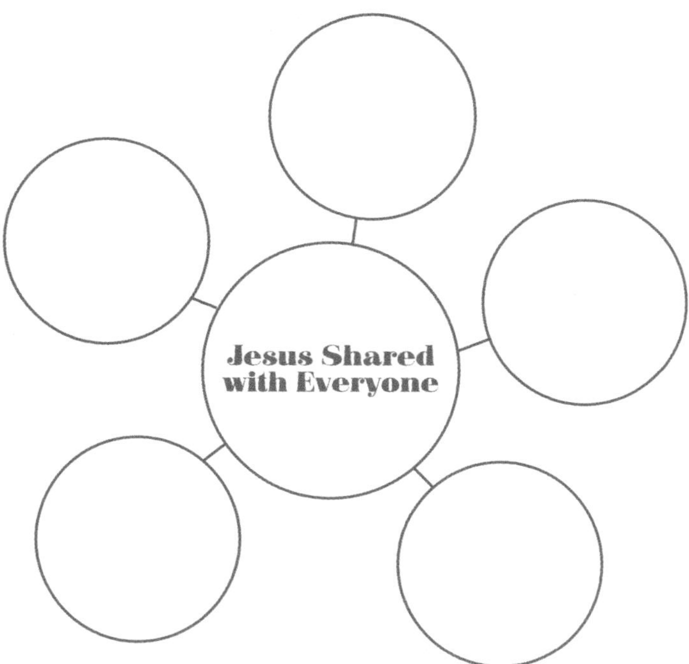

Now, think back to the statement that "the gospel is for everyone." Think about who "everyone" might mean in your own life. List some names and ideas of ways you can minister to those people like Jesus would. If you need help, talk with your parents or youth pastor to determine one way you can commit to serving and sharing the gospel with your "everyone" over the next month.

LIFEWAY STUDENT DEVOTIONS

Engage with God's Word.

lifeway.com/teendevotionals

- [ ] ALREADY BUT NOT YET

- [ ] THE ESSENTIALS

- [ ] CALLED
- [ ] PRESENCE & PURPOSE

- [ ] REVEALED

- [ ] LION OF JUDAH

- [ ] YOUR WILL BE DONE

- [ ] SPIRIT & TRUTH

- [ ] THREE-IN-ONE
- [ ] IN THE BEGINNING

- [ ] TRUTH AND LOVE
- [ ] SEARCH AND KNOW